Carry Me Away

Poems by Matt Goodfellow

Illustrated by Sue Hardy-Dawson

Copyright © 2016 Matt Goodfellow
Illustrations © 2016 Sue Hardy-Dawson

The moral right of the author has been asserted.

Apart from any fair dealing for the purposes of research or private study, or criticism or review, as permitted under the Copyright, Designs and Patents Act 1988, this publication may only be reproduced, stored or transmitted, in any form or by any means, with the prior permission in writing of the publishers, or in the case of reprographic reproduction in accordance with the terms of licences issued by the Copyright Licensing Agency. Enquiries concerning reproduction outside those terms should be sent to the publishers.

This is a work of fiction. Names, characters, businesses, places, events and incidents are either the products of the author's imagination or used in a fictitious manner. Any resemblance to actual persons, living or dead, or actual events is purely coincidental.

Matador
9 Priory Business Park,
Wistow Road, Kibworth Beauchamp,
Leicestershire. LE8 0RX
Tel: 0116 279 2299
Email: books@troubador.co.uk
Web: www.troubador.co.uk/matador
Twitter: @matadorbooks

ISBN 9781785892608

British Library Cataloguing in Publication Data.
A catalogue record for this book is available from the British Library.

Printed and bound by CPI Group (UK) Ltd, Croydon, CR0 4YY

Matador is an imprint of Troubador Publishing Ltd

For Joanna, Will and Daisy

26th May 2016

For Olivia,
Best Wishes
Matt Gaw

About Matt

Matt is a poet and primary school teacher from Manchester. He was supposed to be a rock star until he eventually realised he had absolutely no musical ability whatsoever – the song lyrics he used to write, however, developed into poems. Matt tours the UK visiting schools, libraries, (and anywhere else that will have him) to deliver high-energy, fun-filled poetry performances and workshops.

What people say about Matt's poems:

Carry Me Away blends poems of humour, intrigue and a love for the natural world. They will both challenge and amuse the young reader. This is a promising debut from a contemporary, new voice.

(Rachel Rooney, poet)

Matt is one of the children's poets who will carry the poetry flag in future years. In a genre that is currently lacking in younger writers, Matt can make children smile with his word play, but he can also make them think and wonder.

(Brian Moses, poet & anthologist)

There is a true stroke of originality and brightness about Matt's work.

(Wes Magee, poet)

Matt Goodfellow's poems are brimful of delightful linguistic twists and turns that always lead the reader down fresh and unexpected paths. His imaginative, inventive verses not only leave a strong initial impression but stick long in the memory. A rising star of the children's poetry firmament, Matt is definitely one to watch out for.

(Graham Denton, poet & anthologist)

What people say about Matt's poetry performances and workshops:

Matt's infectious enthusiasm ran right through the school and inspired children and staff alike to read and perform poetry not only in the workshops and performances but beyond. Every single child went away with a smile on their face!

(Matthew Hover, Headteacher, Ashton Hayes Primary School, Cheshire)

Matt engaged the children brilliantly with his lively poetry and his wit. He is both entertaining and inspiring. Children from Foundation Stage to Year 6 loved working with him and teachers were left buzzing with ideas about how to deliver poetry in exciting ways.

(Angela Ridley, Headteacher, Mersey Drive Primary School, Bury)

When your 'hard to reach' boys are searching for Matt, notebooks in hand, to show him their poetry compositions, you know he's getting something right. An inspirational day!

(Paul Heaton, Headteacher, St Mary's RC Primary, Radcliffe)

The best day in school ever!

(Y6 child, St Theresa's RC Primary School, Irlam)

Contact Information

✉ mattgoodfellowpoet@hotmail.com

W www.mattgoodfellow.yolasite.com

Contents

With the Waterfalls	9
When I Swing	10
Ginny Green Teeth	11
Trampoline Dream	12
Musician Wishing	13
Just Words	14
Wasted	15
The New Girl	16
The Shepherd-Boy	17
Mystery	18
Holiday Hideaway	20
A Complaint	21
The Spaeman	22
Puffin	23
Snowem	24
Magic Trick	25
Frustrated Magician	26
My Shell	28
Mermaid	29
Last Night	31
The Girl from the North Side	32
Pebble	33
Murmuration	34
Barometer Boy	35
Thought Cloud	36
Crocodile	37
Another Place	38
The Sorcerer's Tune	39

Carry Me Away	40
Dragon Air	41
Rise	42
Poem for a New Year	43
My Shadow	44
The Old Walker's Song	46
Polar Bear	47
Something's Going Down	48
I Live Inside a Violin	49
The Boy That Came from Under the Ground	51
The Move	53
Poem Growing	54
The Mackerel Girl	55
Michael	56
Up	58
I am a Child	60
Drifting	61
Here it Comes	62
Faffternoon	63
The Witching Hour	64
Snow in the Woods	66
Pelican Curry	67
To This	69
From the Field	70
The Old Farmer's Song	71
Manta Ray	72
Little Luna Latimer	74
Word Hungry	75
Bees in the Brickwork	76
I Wasn't Me Tonight	77

With the Waterfalls

I'm miles away today: I'm with the waterfalls.
I won't be round to play so please don't try to call.

I'm out beyond the boundary in the shimmer-spray.
Thick folds of mist surround me but I know the way.

I've walked towards the roar a thousand times before.
I'm miles away today: I'm with the waterfalls.

When I Swing

When I swing
I seem
to forget
everything

I wash
my mind
in the sky.

Feet first
I burst
this blur
of world

and

fly

        fly

                fly.

Ginny Green Teeth

Ginny Green Teeth is a-hidin' in the water,
Ginny Green Teeth is the Devil's own daughter.

Out among the shallows of the boggy Cheshire plain
underneath the duckweed, there's a demon that's a-layin',
waitin' for a wanderer to step too close and then
pulled into the underworld, they're never seen again.

Ginny Green Teeth is a-hidin' in the water,
Ginny Green Teeth is the Devil's own daughter.

Children of the villages are warned to never play
anywhere near marshy ground or swampy waterway.
When moonlight on the sniddlebog is shining clear and cold
the water-wench is prowling, on the hunt for careless souls.

Ginny Green Teeth is a-hidin' in the water,
Ginny Green Teeth is the Devil's own daughter.

Ginny is a figure from English folklore appearing in traditional stories from Cheshire, Lancashire and Shropshire. She is sometimes called Jinny, Jenny or Jeannie.

Trampoline Dream

I sometimes have this special dream:
I'm bouncing on a trampoline –
then fluid, formless, free of care,
I skim the wind and blend with air.

Musician Wishing

Found a trumpet, drum and whistle
started thinking maybe this'll
be the sign that I should start myself
a one-boy band...

grabbed a banjo from the attic
made a proper pleasing racket
and my mum she must've loved it
'cos she screamed and waved her hands.

All my instruments together
(if I'm careful and I'm clever)
are a guarantee of fortune
who'll propel me to the top.

Now the only thing I'm missing
is an audience who'll listen
to the magic of my music
without begging me to stop...

Just Words

I tasted a word
fiery, hot
loosened a word
from a fisherman's knot

fattened a word
on saucers of cream
quarried a word
got rich on its seam

planted a word
deep in the soil
anointed a word
with ashes and oil

harnessed a word
exploited its power
banished a word
to an ivory tower

polished a word
wore it pinned to my chest
finished a word
with a rattling breath

Wasted

Dad gets piles of newspapers
but never reads a word

Mum's got stacks of records
that she's never even heard

the shed is full of walking boots
they've never even laced

I wouldn't mind but I'm the one
they say's a waste of space

The New Girl

The new girl in class
has a slice of the sky
that she wears on a chain
round her neck

whenever she laughs
it's the finest cyan
but when she's unhappy
it's black

now I know what you're thinking –
it sounds pretty strange
but I'll tell you
what's really bizarre:

whenever I talk
to the new girl in class
her sky-necklace
shimmers with stars

The Shepherd-Boy

away up the fell where the snow's setting in
a shepherd-boy raises his staff to the wind

he calls through the cloud into indigo skies
storm-silhouettes with the fells in their eyes

wade down through the rushes to follow the words
of a shepherd-boy singing the song of his herd

'fell' is a word which means mountain or hill

Mystery

an oilslick-black
cat
is sliding through shadows
that
swallow my
street
on velvety
feet
his tread is
soft
but his body is
taut
night-eyes
glare
drifts like
air
prowling wisp
hell-fire
hiss
flicks an ear
disappears

Holiday Hideaway

Summer days are not for me:
lobster skin, stinging bee,
ice-cream drip, sand-chafed toes,
pollen causing streaming nose.

I'll be snoozing, tucked away –
let others blister as they play!
When sweat and sun cream burn their eyes
I'm on the sofa – safe inside.

So stuff your smoke-choked barbecue,
strawberry stains and tennis, too.
I'm hibernating in my room –
winter rain can't come too soon.

A Complaint

I can
land lightly on leaves
in soft plump
drops

I can
fall in fevered fists
pounding out the oldest
beat of all

I can
coax flowered flares
of life from
a dusty little seed

I can
bend mighty rays of sunlight
to paint the sky
with a rainbow

and what thanks do I get for
my artistry?

a roll of the eyes
a tight-lipped tut
and the tug of a hood

The Spaeman

The Spaeman speaks in riddles
no-one understands,
he sleeps in hidden hovels –
a secret of the land.

He senses seasons changing,
he feels the planets spin,
he sees the truth in daydreams
and patterns in the wind.

He walks beside the river
silently for miles.
The Spaeman speaks in riddles
and smiles and smiles
and smiles.

*'Spaeman' (pronounced Spayman) is an ancient Scottish word meaning,
'a man who can forsee the future; a soothsayer'*

Puffin

if you
flew
mile after mile
across wide shining oceans
on stubby wings like these,
wouldn't you
too
be
puffin?

Snowem

a blink of black
against the white
is leaving tracks
across the night

on frozen fields
here and there
poetry
by moonlit hare

Magic Trick

I can make myself disappear
it's really really easy
I walk into a room
and nobody even sees me

the key to being invisible
is simple and it's free
the only thing you need to do
is sound and look like
me

Frustrated Magician

Wherever I go, whatever I do,
I always end up at the back of a queue.
I queue for the circus, I queue at the till,
I queue at the doctors to tell him I'm ill.

I queue at the sweetshop, I queue for new shoes,
I queue for the dodgems and queue for the loos.
I queue at the football, I queue for my chips,
I queue for the coach when we go on school trips.

I queue up so often, I'm learning a trick
to get to the front of the line double-quick:
I itch and I scratch and start jumping around,
shout, 'Goodness! You'll never believe what I found!

I'm covered! They're biting! ENORMOUS BLACK FLEAS!
Help me! Oh, help me! Won't somebody, please?'
In under a minute, there's nobody there…

And that's how to make all your queues disappear!

My Shell

there is a shell
alone on a beach
over the sand-dunes
out of my reach

it calls to me softly
whispers my name
says, 'come, won't you find me?'
always the same

one day I will see it
half-buried in sand
and hold it up proud
in the palm of my hand

we'll sing of the sun
and the salt and the sea
together forever
just my shell and me

Mermaid

she sings
of stormy sea-caves
and wild black-water drums

she sings
of secret beaches
where tide-swell softly hums

she sings
the lonely harmonies
of waterfalls and streams

she sings
beneath the whirlpools
and starlight of my dreams

Last Night

Last night, in my dreams,
I followed the path
that the moon laid out
on the sea

in pin-striped pyjamas
I strolled past the harbour
just water supporting
my feet

I carried on out
past the rocks and the buoys
beyond all the cliffs
and the coves

out past the lobster-pots
ferries and fancy yachts
onwards and onwards
I strode

until suddenly there
where the sky melts to sea
I stood in the glow
of the moon –

its gentle light shone
to confirm we were one
and I woke with a start
in my room

The Girl from the North Side

the girl from the north side of the hill
thinner than cotton-grass
born with the chill of the dawn in her eyes

walks the moor-tops in a lavender dress
deep in the folds of her moon-purse
is pressed the last of the hawkweed
remnants of sun

the girl from the north side

remembers its song

Pebble

In silver songs
from river's throat
I am just a tiny note.
But sculpted-smooth
sure, am I,
rounded
ringing
pure and high.

Murmuration

winter dusk
starling flock
living smoke
drifts across
charcoal tree
copper sky
every feather
synchronised

Barometer Boy

I'm weather-clever, me,
a skill unique and strange –
I know before the satellites
when things are set to change.

My body's climate-sensitive,
it's always been the same –
if both my little-toes go green,
I forecast heavy rain.

If I sprout thick sideburns
and a neatly-trimmed moustache,
prepare yourself for thunderstorms
that roll and rage and clash.

If my tongue is itchy
and swamped with swollen spots,
slap the sun-cream on, my dear,
the outlook's roasting-hot.

And if a buttock swells
ballooning like a dinghy,
batten down the hatches, boys,
things are turning windy.

But my favourite's when my fingers
start tingling and glow
for then I know the sky will soon
be filled with falling snow.

Thought Cloud

Throw a rope 'round a cloud,
heave it on down –
what might be found inside?

a fallen angel's wing
postcards from the wind
a torn red kite
pieces of the night

an air-hostess's nail
frozen vapour trails
a pterodactyl tooth
a parachute's whoosh

a solid silver harp
one dark star
a lock of moon-white hair
and
a pilot's last prayer

Crocodile

My skin is as gnarled as a knobbly tree
but my bite is much worse than my bark.
Come snooping too close to my watering hole
and I'll smuggle you into the dark –

where I'll wrestle the breath
from your chest in the depths
and soften you under a rock.

Cold-blooded killer
a flesh-tearing thriller –
I'm merciless, murderous
Croc.

Another Place

Through the mist
on the beach
in a long black coat

he will walk
with the stars
and the note she wrote

looking out
to the place
where she slipped his hand.

And they dance
every night
on the cold wet sand.

The Sorcerer's Tune

I will teach you the knowledge of forest and herb,
I will teach you the magic of stone.
I will teach you the secrets of silence and sound
and the limits of muscle and bone.

I will teach you the power of darkness and light,
I will teach you the wisdom of tree.
I will teach you to dowse for a pathway within,
I will teach you to peacefully see.

I will teach you a journey of healing and hurt,
I will teach you of circle and rune.
I will teach you the forces of season and time,
I will sing you The Sorcerer's Tune.

Carry Me Away

carry me away
on the curve of a shell
to shouldering shingle
and soft-rolling swell

carry me away
on the curve of a wave
to silent horizons
where silver fish blaze

carry me away
on the curve of a swift
to a slow-breaking dawn
in the shimmering mist

Dragon Air

Hello young man and welcome
to this flight with Dragon Air,
the fastest way to travel
and the best thing – there's no fare!

That's right; no money, gratis, free!
So climb up on my back.
Relax and thank your lucky stars…
My Little In-Flight Snack.

Rise

The end of our school field
where the grass grows long
is where I sometimes hide
when the world is going wrong

I lie amongst the dandelions
staring at the sky
wishing I was someone else
wishing I could fly

out into the atmosphere
swooping through the clouds
somewhere much less complicated
somewhere much less loud

somewhere safe and peaceful
where all secrets are revealed
I close my eyes, become the skies
and rise above this field

Poem for a New Year

Something's moving in,
I hear the weather in the wind,
sense the tension of the sheep-field
and the pilgrimage of fins.

Something's not the same,
I taste the sap and feel the grain,
hear the rolling of the rowan
ringing, singing in a change.

Something's set to start,
there's meadow-music in the dark
and the clouds that shroud the mountain
slowly, softly start to part.

My Shadow

My shadow's as sad
as a shadow can be
we are deeply attached
yet he dreams to be free

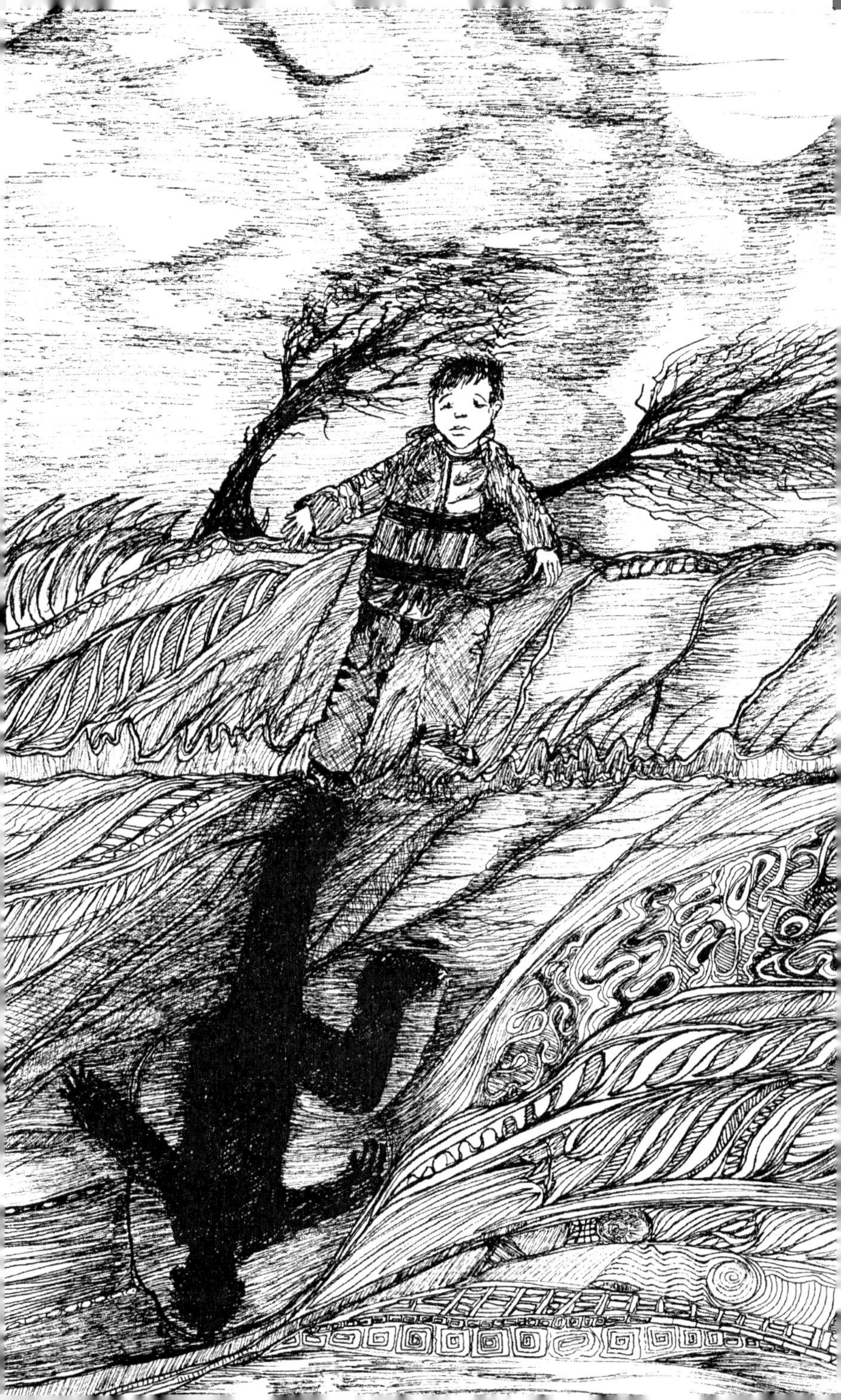

The Old Walker's Song

Goodbye to wide horizons,
the Pennine peaks, my home.
Rucksack, tent and sleeping bag
were all I'd need to roam.

Lapwing over limestone,
red grouse in the spring,
adders in the bracken –
land of everything.

But waterproofs have faded.
Boots lie long un-waxed.
I walk in mist-swim memories
of wind-blast moorland tracks.

I understand the cycle,
the singer and the song –
this is the way it needs to be:
the hills are moving on.

Polar Bear

An iceberg of urges
patrolling pack-ice

with jack-hammer paws
and incisors to slice

is searching the snow
for the scent of a seal –

awesome aggression
in need of a meal.

A blizzard of fur
with a predator stare:

carnivore king,
the polar bear.

Something's Going Down

a pair of shifty-looking foxes skirt
the long shadows in the meadow

a flock of starlings whisper conspiratorially
in the oak trees

the daisies have hidden their faces

and

a bat opens an eye

there's definitely something going down
around here

I Live Inside a Violin

I live inside a violin
(I'm really rather small)
I play the music that you hear
the notes, the tune – it all.

Life has certain compromises
(lack of space and things)
but it's handy hanging washing
on the integrated strings.

We travel all around the world
my violin and me –
proof that two can live as one
in perfect harmony.

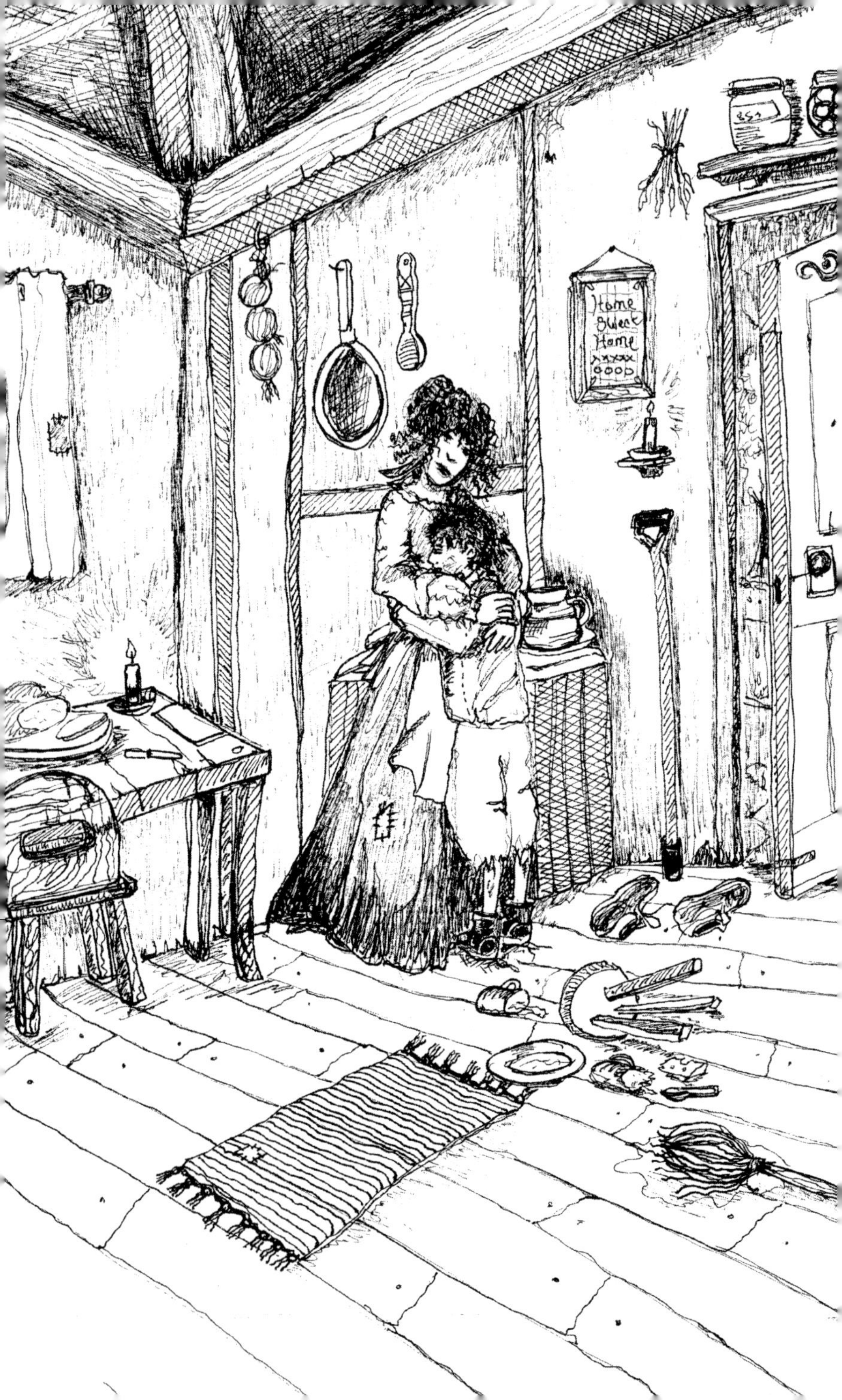
Home
Sweet
Home

The Boy That Came from Under the Ground

The boy that came from under the ground
swears by the stars he was stolen, not found.

Plucked from his dreams in the moor where he lay,
rudely unearthed and then carried away.

Washed at the fire by a peat-cutter's wife,
he pleaded with her: *'I am not of this life.*

Your milk burns my stomach; the sun burns my eyes.
I am born of the darkness where thunderous skies

meet cliff-top and cavern below flaming peaks,
I was lost and confused when you tore me from sleep.

Unless you release me, destruction and ill
will tear down this cottage – I swear that it will!'

But the peat-cutter's wife always longed for a child,
she dressed him up handsome, she kissed him and smiled:

'This is your home now, stop making a fuss,
You're a peat-cutter's lad and you'll stay here with us.'

His sadness grew stronger the longer he stayed,
through autumn and spring and the hot summer days.

Till one winter night, with the cottage asleep,
the boy gazed up moonwards and started to weep.

The tears that he shed soaked into the ground
and deep from the depths came a splintering sound;

cracks opened up in the fields all around.
The world started shaking, the roof tumbled down.

The cottage collapsed with a sickening lurch,
swallowed by blackness, consumed by the earth.

He stood there a minute. In silence. Alone.
Then climbed into darkness and headed for home.

This poem is based on the folk tale, 'The Boy who Came from the Ground' which originates from the Shetland Isles.

The Move

On the day we finally left,
when the new family's van arrived

I swallowed the sharpest of breaths.
Kissed each wall. And cried.

Poem Growing

Poem growing's easy
in the garden of your mind,
just a little thinking
sprouts ideas of every kind.
Germinate, cultivate,
prune whenever needed
and given time
they'll bloom just fine – Hey Presto! –
you've succeeded!

The Mackerel Girl

The last time that I saw her
she was wading out to sea,
singing: 'Come with me my brother,
let the both of us be free.

They are waiting in the moonlight,
steel-bellied every one,
they have listened to me, brother.
They have listened, they have come!'

As she turned to face me one last time,
she waved a marbled hand
and she weaved beneath the water
and she left me on the land.

Michael

Michael fell asleep in class last week,
face down on the desk.
Spark out in the middle of maths.
Mr Jones told us off for laughing, but
didn't seem cross with him at all;

Michael plays alone at break.
He just stands, staring into space,
watching the sky. Looking odd.
But the teacher on duty always goes
over and chats to him.
They never do that for us.

Michael only has a biscuit in his lunchbox
most days so the cook gives him stuff
for free;

Michael never takes his shoes and socks off
even when we do gym or dance
and Mr Jones lets him –
we all have to do it barefoot;

Michael gets loads of stickers
and certificates off all the adults
whenever he does anything.

Once, Leah swears she saw the Head,
Mrs Malone, wipe away a tear after she'd
seen his book and he'd only written a sentence;

Michael must be really lucky.

Up

Up at the top
of the very big hill
cloud-covered valleys
held everything still.
I knew then and there
that the climb had been worth it –
and just for a moment
the whole world was

perfect

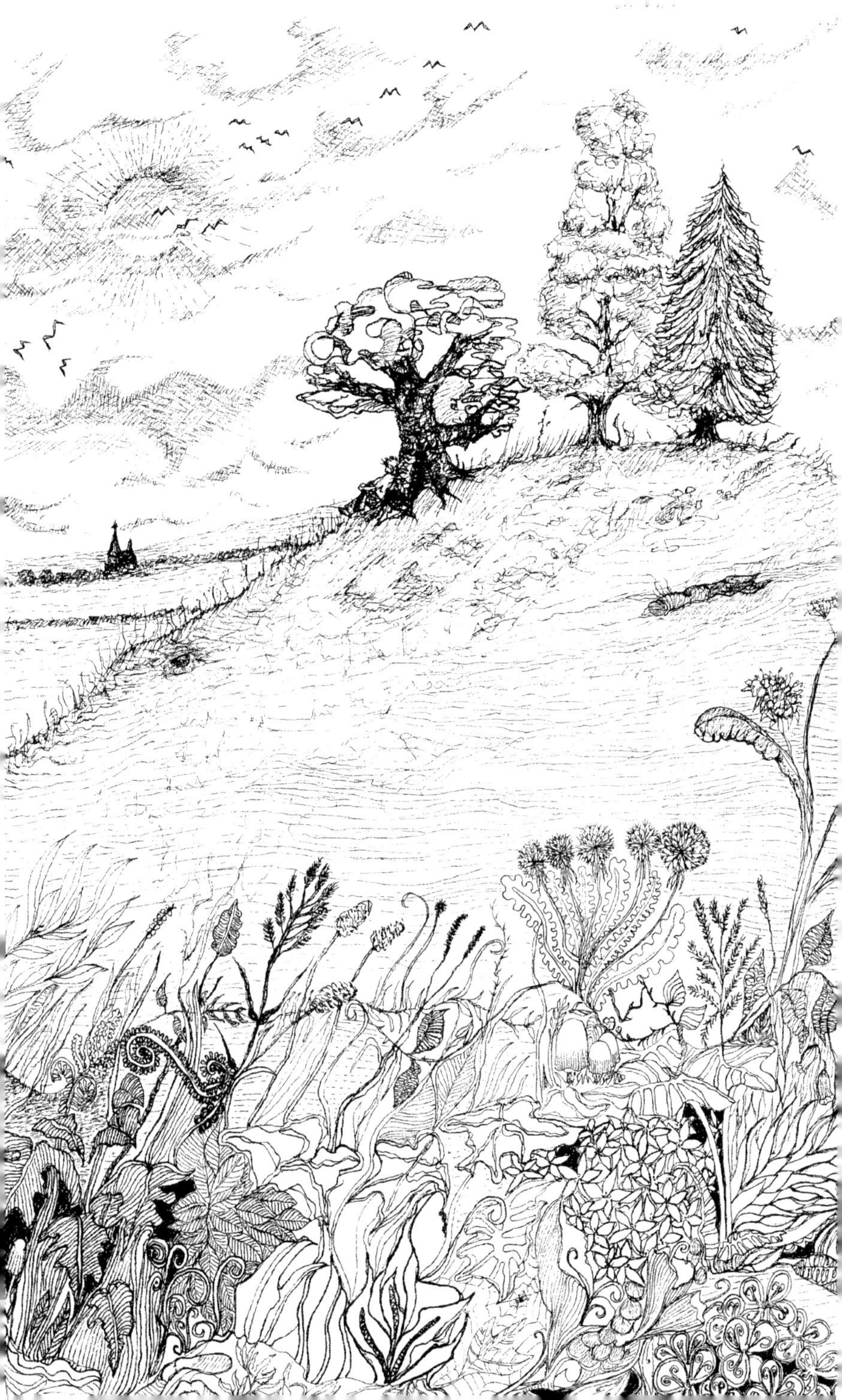

I am a Child

I am a child
who slips through the net
never a bully
not teacher's pet.

I am a child
on the edge of the crowd
sometimes too quiet
never too loud.

I am a child
who causes no fuss
not one to dawdle
not one to rush.

But I am a child
with tears in my eyes
drifting unnoticed
lost to the tide.

Drifting

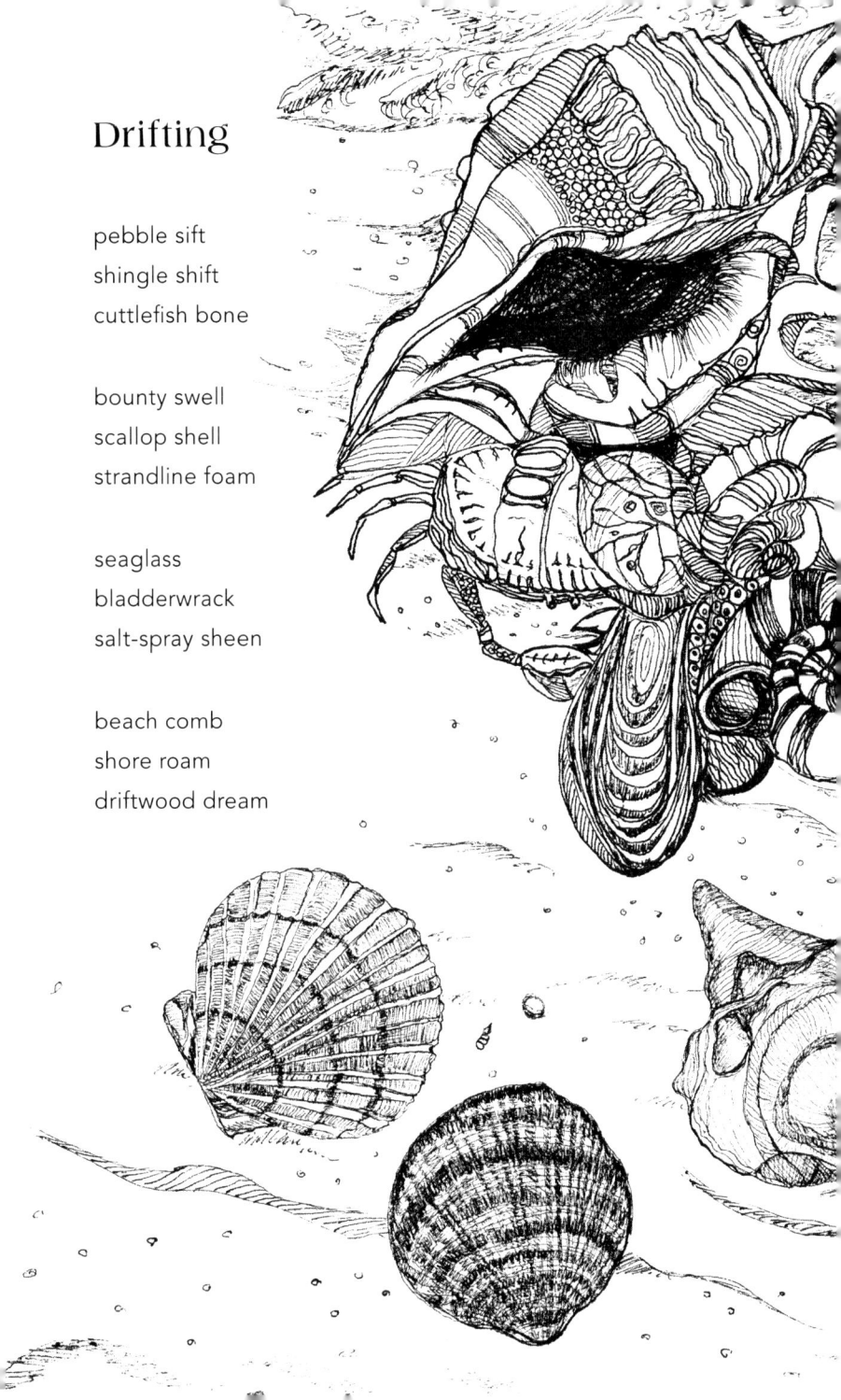

pebble sift
shingle shift
cuttlefish bone

bounty swell
scallop shell
strandline foam

seaglass
bladderwrack
salt-spray sheen

beach comb
shore roam
driftwood dream

Here it Comes

Hunker down
snow's in town
dressing gown
bed.

Morning light
snowball fight
shining bright
sled.

Fafternoon

When it's really, really, really hot
and there's really not an awful lot
of work to do and it's holidays soon,
we have what's called a Fafternoon.

We put our writing books away,
chill out, unwind, relax and play.
No mental maths. No reading test.
No targets met. No spelling stress.

No algebra. No grammar gloom.
Just a summer Fafternoon.

The Witching Hour

The stones speak to me, here.
Fallen pine-cones hum.
The moon spills silver on the path.
The witching hour has come.

Ancient incantation.
Song of shadow-tongue.
A creeping chill cuts through the earth.
The witching hour has come.

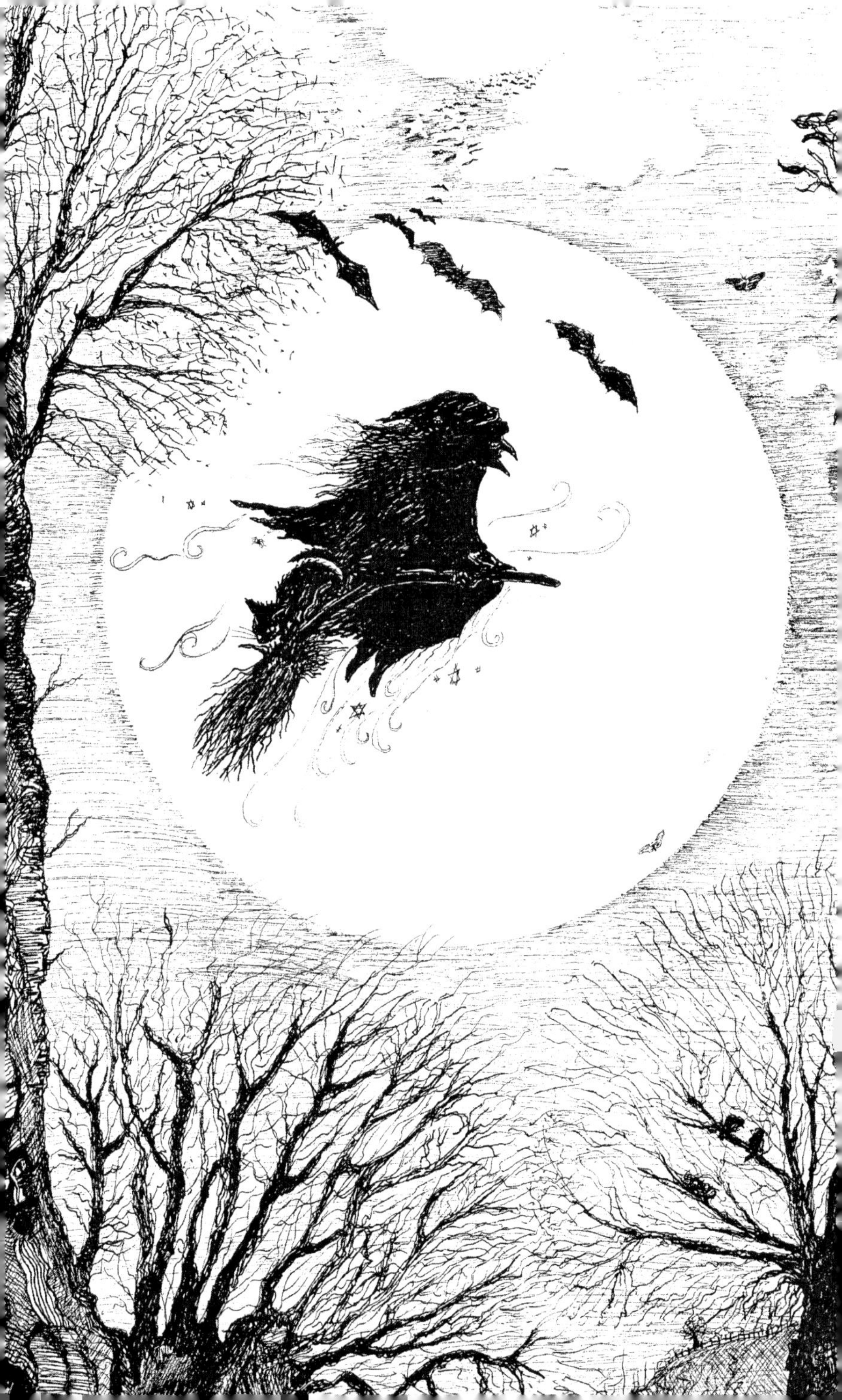

Snow in the Woods

Bare
bear.

Brrr.

Pelican Curry

A pelican curry
is a hot and spicy thrill,
the only real problem –
the whacking great bill!

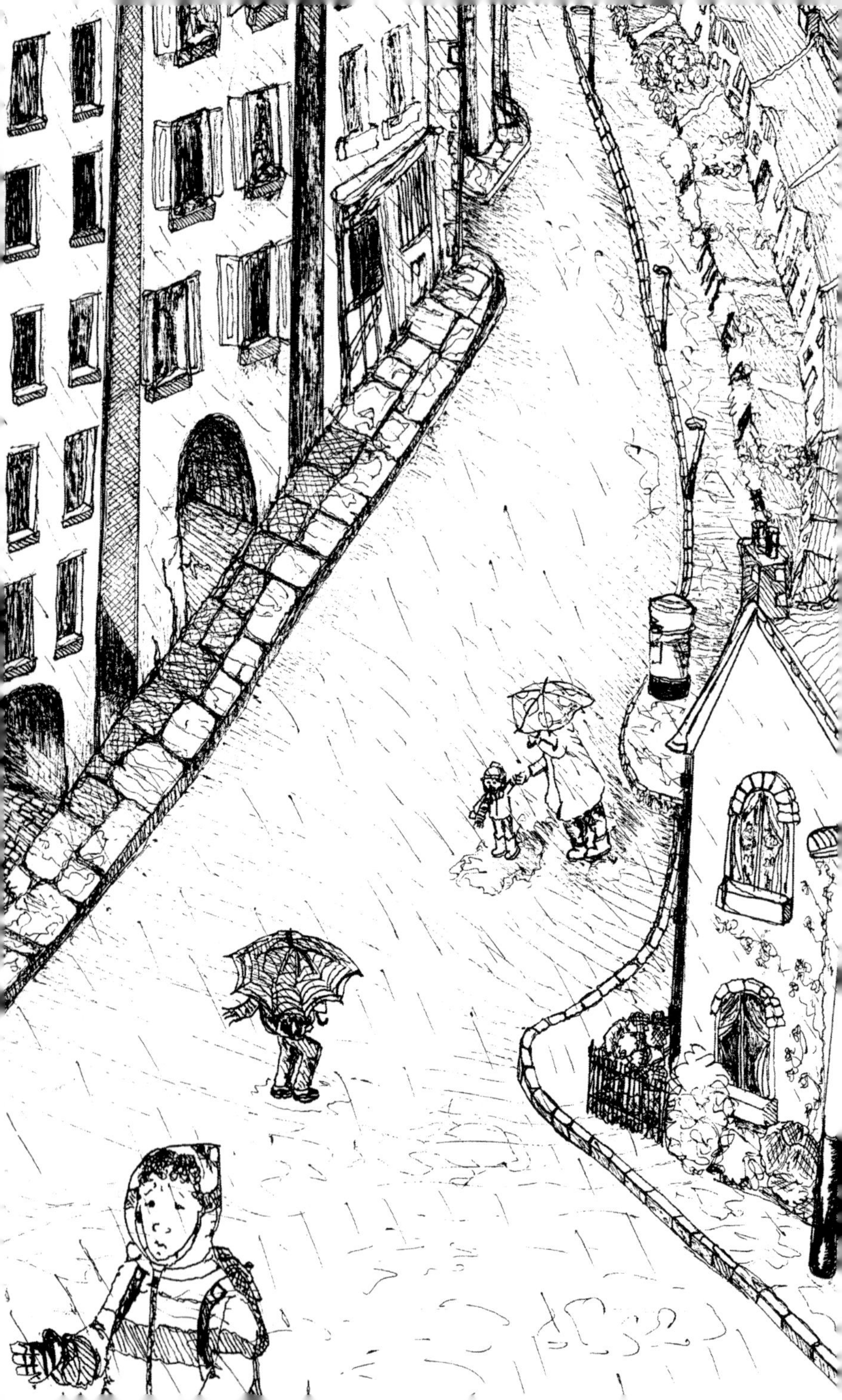

To This

I came with nothing
but the Mediterranean in my eyes
and a knot in my stomach

to this

concrete chaos
rainy streets
icy looks
burning cheeks

dad
on the balcony
waving
as we
drove away

to this

to this

From the Field

Father, top-field is furrowed,
there's nowt not been turned by the plough,
old Elsie is settled and watered –
I've a full day of sweat on me brow!

But why do I find you bewildered
with cheeks gone the colour of chalk?
Your dark eyes are hooded and frightened,
loosen your tongue, Father, talk!

My boy, what I utter, forgive me,
is spoken in torment, not fear:
it's a cruel kind of pleasure to see you,
my only born son, standing here

with shoulders still strong as an oak tree
while I have grown withered and old –
for ten bitter winters have passed, Jack,
since you laid on this table-top…cold.

The Old Farmer's Song

At the edge of the world I graze my sheep
where storm-clouds swirl and the valley cuts deep.

I've farmed this land for fifty years,
calloused my hands on shovels and shears,

raised my cattle as best I could,
a constant battle in thick bog mud.

But a soaring hawk, a hare on the run,
an early walk with the rising sun,

a horse's flanks as they heave and steam,
frost on the banks of a snow-melt stream

makes my old heart beat to the rhythm of the farm,
the low pig grunts and the cows in the barn.

Till I'm ash and dust, when I'm dead and gone,
I'll be in these hills, and I'll sing this song.

Manta Ray

manta ray
breath of sea
wing-tips whisper
mystery

ocean shadow
floating kite
somersaulting
hood of night

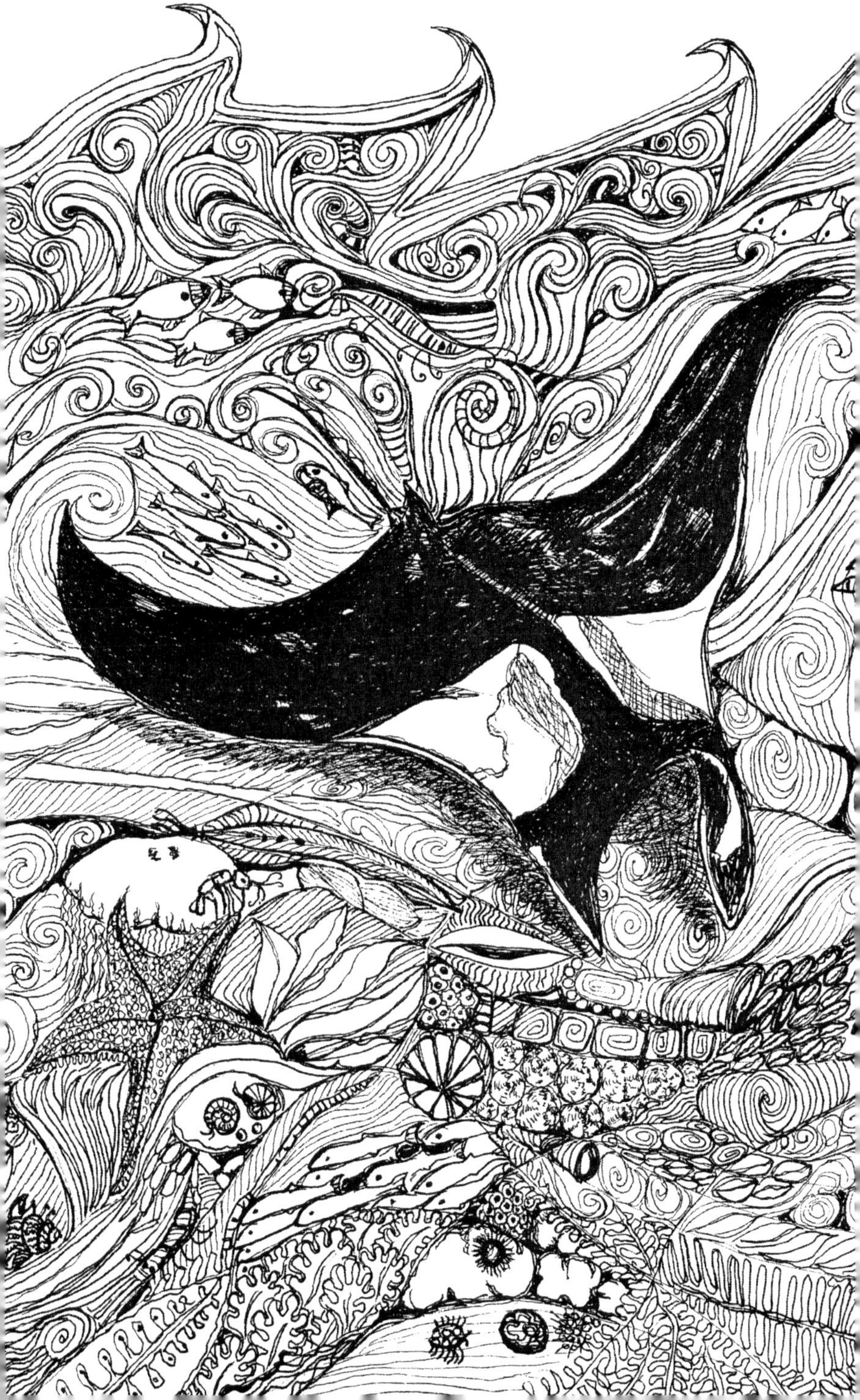

Little Luna Latimer

When Luna
breathed mist-patches
on the bus window
and smeared squeaky shapes
with her thumb,
mum leaned in close:
don't do that, Luna, she said.

When Luna
scratched symbols
into frost on the car-bonnet
with her fingernails,
dad beeped the horn:
don't do that, Luna, he said.

When Luna
picked rose-petals
and piled them into patterns
on the grass,
grandma wagged a finger:
don't do that, Luna, she said.

But little Luna Latimer
still undeterred, it seems,
continues seeking canvasses
on which to draw her dreams.

Word Hungry

this is a pomegranate

this is a poemgranate

this is a poem gran ate

burp

Bees in the Brickwork

there are bees
        in the brickwork
I hear them
        scrape their wings
beneath cracks
        in swollen plaster
more and more
        keep stealing in
I can feel them
        honey-veining
little feet
        burn everything
there are bees
        in the brickwork
they are growing

they will win

I Wasn't Me Tonight

I was a liquorice black
velvet bat, arcing and
wheeling at twilight

slicing through the thin air
silent as silk.
My tight-skinned wings
stretched out against

the blossoming moon.

Many thanks to all those who have supported me on the journey to arrive here.

Extra special thanks to Sue Hardy-Dawson for her advice, kindness and genius with a pen and ink! Sue has been widely published in children's poetry anthologies and long listed for the 2014 Manchester Writing for Children Prize. She has an open First Class Honours Degree and has provided workshops, both in schools and for the Foundation for Children and the Arts. As a dyslexic poet, she is especially interested in encouraging reluctant readers and writers.

http://suehd1963.wix.com/author-blog

Thanks also to Kelly Alderdice from 2Ten Graphic Design for her generosity and tireless hard work with the layout of this book.

2Ten Graphic Design *2TenGraphicDesign@gmail.com*

- Matt Goodfellow

Acknowledgements

Matt would like to thank the editors of the following books/magazines where some of these poems previously appeared:

'Something's Going Down' 'I am a Child' and 'Holiday Hideaway' from *The Scrumbler*, ed. Michael Kavanagh

'Frustrated Magician' 'Dragon Air' and 'The Boy That Came From Under the Ground' from *The Caterpillar*, ed. Rebecca O'Connor

'Ginny Green Teeth' from *Falling Out of the Sky*, ed. Rachel Piercey and Emma Wright, The Emma Press

'The Old Farmer's Song' from *Dear Tomato*, ed. Carol-Ann Hoyte

'When I Swing' from *Off By Heart,* ed. Roger Stevens, A&C Black

'Pelican Curry' from *The Silly Book of Weird and Wacky Words*, by Andy Seed, Bloomsbury

'Another Place' and 'With the Waterfalls' from *Let in the Stars*, ed. Mandy Coe, The Manchester Writing School

'A Complaint' and 'I wasn't me tonight' from *A First Poetry Book*, ed. Pie Corbett and Gaby Morgan, Macmillan

'Puffin' 'Poem Growing' and 'Manta Ray' from *Orbit – The School Magazine*, Australia